YOUR FREE GIFT

Thanks for buying my book!

As a way of showing my appreciation, I'd like to give a **FREE bonus gifts** exclusive to my readers.

I've created a special FREE PDF CHEAT SHEET of:

"Everything You Need to Know to Check Your Credit Score" and a FREE PDF CHECKLIST of:

"15 Things That You Can Do To Improve Your Credit Score"

The Cheat Sheet will guide you with an easy, step-by-step way to check your credit score and the Checklist will show you a list of simple, practical things that you can do to improve your credit score drastically!

Get it Here:

https://BookHip.com/BFBFTT

TABLE OF CONTENTS

Smart Personal Money
Management Series - Book 2

ALL ABOUT

CREDIT

SMART MONEY SECRET

A Beginner's Step-by-Step Guide to Understanding How Credit Works and How to Build Up Your **Credit Score**

by
Rachel Mercer

COPYRIGHT AND DISCLOSURES

INTRODUCTION

Hi!!
So, you're here.
Still a little bit unsure if this is really the spot for you, but you're here.

Well. That's already a huge first step :)

And let me guess...

You're going, like, is this whole credit score thing really so big?

I mean, what gives? I've managed just fine without it so far...

But there's that niggling little thought at the back of your mind, isn't there?

Whispering in your ear that maybe you're missing out on something pretty important with this credit score business.

And that's why you're here.

Gotta tell you, that niggling little voice is right.

That credit score? It *CAN* change your life. Literally.

It can make some things *sooooo* much easier and cheaper (I got your attention there, didn't I now? Hah!).

But it can also make you want to stick your head in the sand like an ostrich.

Wait, what??

Pffft. I've made it this far just fine, and I ain't never spent a dime trying to work out my credit score!

Okay. It's great that you haven't run into any trouble so far.

I'm really, *really* happy for you on that account.

But give me just a moment here. There's no running away from the bottom line, and it's very simple.

Is This Book For You?

Unless you're a multi-millionaire and can buy whatever you want with a snap of your fingers, you'll just have to face that credit score someday. Sooner, rather than later.

And the way I see it, when that time comes, it's better to be ready for it, right?

Your credit score is a bit like a coin. You got a good credit score, you come up heads.

That house loan you wanted? What do you know, the bank will give it to you, and even offer a lower interest rate. Even your car insurer may give you a better deal.

And that's just the tip of the iceberg.

But a bad credit score? Oops, tails.

That job you nearly nailed? Slipped away at the last moment. And that awesome condo you wanted to rent? Well, it suddenly became unavailable.

And there's many more folks that can complicate your life if they don't like your credit score.

Now I don't want to scare you, but that's just the way the system works.

A lot of people in a lot of places will let your credit score decide how helpful they're gonna be.

So if you're looking for clean, solid answers on exactly what your credit score is and what you can do with it, you're totally in the right place.

I wrote this book for people. I mean *people*, not finance geeks and financial news editors that speak economic tongue-twisters faster than I can think them :)

I'm not going to waste your time with long, boring explanations of the principles behind the principles.

I know I wouldn't put up with that, and I don't expect you to either...:)

So I'll just get right down to it, and explain the what, how, and why.

I'll tell you everything it makes sense to know about your credit score, and how you can make it work for you.

There's a lot of myth around credit scores, and I'll unravel it, step by step.

If you want to know how a great credit score can help you, I'll tell you.

And best of all, I'll show you exactly what you can do to raise it.

I'm Not a Credit Score Newbie, What's In It For Me?

 Okay. So you're savvy, and you know what a credit score is and what it can do for you (or to you).

And that's awesome, coz not everyone does. In fact, credit scores are wrapped in myth for so many people.

But here's the thing.

Some things about your credit score can seem straightforward at first glance. But when you dig a little bit deeper, you may discover that it's not quite what your lender (or collecting agency) would have you believe.

And it's understanding the finer details that can get your score going from good to excellent.

Just like that. If your score is already good, then you're doing stuff right.

But sometimes, it's about beating the system at its own game.

Don't worry, I'm not peddling any illegal tricks here.

All I'm doing is showing you exactly how to get the system to work to your advantage, instead of the other way round.

I'll brag just a little and tell you that my current credit score is 829.

But believe you me, it wasn't always nearly that good.

It took me a while to get the fine-tuning sorted. But I did it, and I want to share the how with *you*.

In my experience, no matter how much you know, there's always more.

And I think that as you go through the chapters of this book, you'll find yourself a couple of 'Aha!' moments.

Sometimes, all it takes is one or two game-changing nuggets of info to get that credit score going where you need it.

And that's up, up, up.

What This Book Really Teaches You

If you've made it this far, then I hope I've convinced you that your credit score is worth settling your score with. Pun intended :)

What I want is to give you simple, straightforward ways you can raise your credit score.

And it doesn't matter how good or bad it is right now. There's *always* something you can do to get it better.

But I didn't know a thing about credit scores when I started out. I wish someone had been there to explain it to me. In clear, simple English.

So that's what I'm going to do here.

I'm going to start with the basics, and explain just what your credit score is, and what goes into making it.

Great.

But what's the point of knowing all that if you don't know what your current credit score is??

It may be scary, but you've got to take the plunge at some point…

So then I'll show you nifty little ways you can estimate your credit score.

And I'll even tell you how you can get the real deal for free.

I'm thinking, by now you'll know exactly why a great credit score is great.

And you'll know your own score. So being the smart person that you are, you'll be wanting to get it as high as you can. As fast as you can.

So then we get to the really cool stuff.

I'll show you a bunch of simple but effective things you can do to get your score skyrocketing. And most of this stuff, you'll be able to do as you read along.

I'm not into bombarding you with mind-boggling theory. All I'm after is showing you practical ways to quickly get your credit score going up. No matter your current situation.

Some of the stuff in here may surprise you, even if you already know something about credit scores.

But hey, life's full of surprises, right..? :)

So grab a cuppa, and dive right in. I'll do my best to leave you wide awake and smiling by the time you're done... :)

CHAPTER 1
DOES A BAD CREDIT SCORE REALLY AFFECT ME?

Oh, yes. It does. Ask Me Why.

You don't know much about a credit score except that it exists?
And you've managed to coast along just fine so far?

You're really, really lucky.

It's a good thing you haven't run into any not-so-pleasant situations.

And not to scare you, but sometimes things can get untoward when your credit score is less than shiny.

The long and short of it is this: A bad credit score tells people they can't trust you with their money.

Hey, I work for my own money, you might say.

Of course! And it's definitely up to you how you spend your hard-earned cash.

But what about those times when you need a little something in advance? You know you'll get your paycheck at the end of the month, but you wanted that something *now.*

It might be that funky mobile phone you've been coveting, and it's finally on sale, but only for today. Or maybe it's a great deal at that classy new salon, and you don't want to miss out.

Okay, so this is stuff that you *can* do without.

No big deal.

But when you want something bad...

Well. I know I've succumbed to these kinds of temptations, more than once.

Now let's get serious.

What about those situations when you found something really, really important? Like your dream house, or the perfect wedding gown? These are the kind of expenses most of us can't afford to pay upfront.

So the only way you're going to be able to buy what you want is to get some kind of loan.

Nobody likes taking a big loan, but sometimes it's just unavoidable.

Other times it is, totally. It's not a case of life or death (or is it..? :).

Like when you want a total makeover at that new spa or those fancy rims for your car...:)

But you want it sooooo bad, you just don't care. You'll want some quick cash anyway.

And THAT's where your credit score comes knocking.

That new credit card you wanted? If your credit score is not spick and span, you just might not get it.

The dream home you wanted to buy? Your banker will politely shut their door in your face if they don't like your credit score.

And there's so many more things a bad credit score can do, none of them very pleasant.

What a Bad Credit Score Does to You in Practical Terms

Like I said, I'm not going to waste your time. Let's take the proverbial bull by the horns, and get the nasty out of the way first.

You wanted to know why it's important to have a good credit score? Here's the big ways how a bad one can affect your life.

Getting a Large, Long-Term Loan Can Become Impossible

Let's face it.

Sooner or later, you'll be wanting something that you can't pay for upfront, so your only option is to take a loan.

And this is usually the important stuff in your life. Student loans, weddings, home improvement loans, buying a new house.

Then there's stuff nobody wants to think about, but it still happens. Like hospital bills and funerals.

The first thing your banker is going to look at is your credit score. If it's very poor, they'll simply refuse to give you the loan. An average credit score will get you that loan, but with a higher interest rate than a good score would have.

New Lines of Credit Become Inaccessible

The way life goes, we usually start looking for access to credit when times get hard.

So if you have a bad credit score, you may end up cutting off access to a credit card when you need it the most.

The credit card provider will not trust you to be able to pay your balances at the end of the month if your credit history is not in top shape.

Your New Job May Slip Away

This one often surprises people. Your potential employer can look at your credit score??

True, they need your permission to do it. But most definitely yes, they can.

Let's get real.

You made it through the gruelling interviews, and you're about to cinch the job. Then the HR guy asks you if they can look at your credit score, and you politely say no, cold sweat pouring down your back.

There goes that new job you've been hoping for. Just because your credit score isn't up to scratch.

Insurance Premiums Can Quickly Get Higher

This is another one that doesn't often occur to people. But it's true.

Insurance companies will frequently look at your credit score before deciding on what to offer you. And it doesn't matter what you're looking for: car insurance, home owner's insurance, and even life insurance.

A good credit score tells the insurer you're careful with your money, and you have a history of managing your finances well. This likely means you can be trusted to manage the rest of your life responsibly as well.

And a bad credit score says the exact opposite. They'll still give you that insurance you wanted. But you'll be paying a higher premium for it.

Accessing Utilities Becomes Harder

All the conveniences we take for granted, like water, electricity, and phone connections, rely on creditworthiness.

In short. If your credit score is bad, you'll either have to pay a deposit on your utilities, or have a co-signer with a good credit score. Just because the provider doesn't trust you to be able to pay your bills.

Legal Affairs Can Become More Complicated

This is an area that if we're lucky, we never have to deal with. But life is unpredictable.

Any time you're involved in any kind of legal altercation, your credit score may be checked. The courts and various government agencies have the right to check your credit score when they think it's necessary.

A simple example is child custody decisions. If you have a bad credit score, you're telling people you have a questionable financial history. The court may rule against you because it doesn't think you're financially capable of taking care of your kids.

Fixing Your Credit Score = Greater Financial Freedom

Not the nicest of things, a bad credit score.

And you may not realize how much trouble it can cause until you find yourself in a situation.

But there's a silver lining to the cloud. You CAN fix your credit score.

And it's not rocket science either. I'm going to show you just how in a bit.

Maybe you know your current score, and it's not bad. Not excellent, but not bad either.

Well, if you're still asking why you should fix it, I'll tell you.

It's simple.

The better your credit score, the more favorably everybody that sees it looks at you.

Simple, but profound.

So when times get hard, you'll have a measure of financial security.

Because official institutions and service providers trust that you'll do your best to recover and pay up your bills when the time comes.

The Benefits of an Excellent Financial Score

An excellent credit score can really open doors. You may even find yourself receiving hush-hush credit offers from your banker, reserved for the select few.

There's a lot an excellent credit score can do.

Let's list it in black and white.

You can get cheaper loans.

Your lender will trust that you know how to manage your finances. They will likely give you the full amount you asked for, and you'll be getting a lower interest rate to boot. So that dream wedding or dream house can finally become yours.

Housing becomes more accessible.

Landlords often check your credit score too. An excellent one assures them of your ability to pay your rent, and you'll be getting that crib you really wanted.

You'll be paying lower insurance premiums.

Be it insurance on your health or car, you're likely to get it at a lower premium if your credit score is all shiny.

Utilities become a breeze.

Even the service providers don't question you much once they assure themselves of your excellent credit score. You'll just sign your contract instead of making deposits and looking for co-signatories.

Jobs can become more accessible.

If you're just looking to wash dishes at a fast-food joint, no one cares. But many higher-paying and more sensitive jobs do require you to have a good credit score.

New lines of credit are easy to get.

If you ever do want a new credit card, you're much more likely to get it hassle-free if your credit score is excellent.

So there you have it. I really wasn't making stuff up..:)

Your credit score *does* matter.

And a good one will take you places, while a bad one can simply shut doors in your face.

So now that you know this stuff is for real, I bet you're itching to figure out how to get your credit score soaring.

Hold your horses just a little bit ..:) !

Let's first work out exactly what a credit score is and who its high-and-mighty makers are. *Then* we'll roll up our sleeves and get down to work.

CHAPTER 2
EXACTLY WHAT IS
A CREDIT SCORE?

How Credit Scores are Calculated

Now you know just how mighty that little number can be, you'll want it shooting up faster than a rocket.

And the great news is that calculating your credit score really isn't rocket science. Pun intended :) It's actually quite simple.

See, no matter who is calculating your credit score (don't worry, we'll get to this in a mo), they're not going to be doing the donkeywork themselves. Oh no.

They're going to use a nifty little algorithm to get the work done for them. All they gotta do is feed it a few values, and it does the rest.

Now I know you're smart, so I'm guessing you've already worked it out.

It all comes down to what is being fed into that algorithm. Period.

And here's the list:

Your payment history is exactly what you think it is. It's a record of all the payments you have ever made on all of your loans, past and present. (Yep, it's not just your banker that keeps track of these things!)

Credit Utilization is just a fancy way of explaining how much of your available credit you are actually using. It's usually expressed in percentage.

So, say, if all your credit cards combined allow you to use a maximum of $10k, and you have used $3k, then your credit utilization is 30%.

The length of your credit history also gets looked at when calculating your credit score. A longer credit history is generally better. That is, of course, if it's a good one, with no late payments and other score-killing stuff.

New credit can also affect your score. Sometimes, getting a new credit card can up your score by a few points. But don't rush to get a new credit card just yet!

Opening a new line of credit is a two-sided coin. Hang on till you get through chapters 5 and 6 before deciding if this is a good alternative for you.

Credit Mix is simply about how many different kinds of loans you have. It may sound counterintuitive, but sometimes, having several different (well-managed!!) loans at once can take your credit score up a notch or two.

These five things are usually what matters the most when calculating your credit score. But there are exceptions.

In some cases, other factors may be considered too. This could be stuff like your utility and rental payments, or public record information, like mortgages and property titles.

So what is used when?

There's actually more than one credit scoring system in use, and each one uses its own proprietary algorithm.

Some systems use the list we just went through, while others ignore it altogether and use the other stuff (utility bills and public records). And others make a potpourri, mixing in a little bit of everything.

Confused much?

Don't be. There are many credit scoring systems, true, but the main one you need to worry about is usually FICO.

What's FICO??

Read on.

FICO and Other Credit Scoring Systems Explained

FICO (used to be the Fair Isaac Corporation) is the most popular credit scoring system in the US today. More than 90% of credit institutions rely on FICO to supply them with the credit scores they want.

FICO uses the five components from our list above to calculate your credit score. But it doesn't treat them equally. Take a look:

Factor Affecting FICO score	How Much It Contributes, %
Payment History	35
Credit Utilization	30
Length of Credit History	15
New Credit	10
Credit Mix	10

As you can see, your payment history and how you use your credit together make for a cool 65% of your total credit score. The other three are minor by comparison.

Quick spoiler: want to raise your credit score? Start with these two!!

VantageScore is another credit scoring system in widespread use and is a direct competitor to FICO. Vantage uses the same five components as FICO but weights them differently. It also uses a different algorithm.

So beware. **FICO** and **VantageScore** may use the same five things to calculate your credit score, but could come up with two wildly different results!

Both systems are well-accepted by the financial community, though. Sometimes, a banker may pull up both reports to decide if they like you enough to lend you their cash.

There are other scoring systems in use besides these two, such as CE Analytics. But these are nowhere as popular, and rarely used when compared to FICO.

Chances are you'll be facing FICO every time the word credit score is mentioned. So, for the rest of this book, we'll focus on the FICO system.

But much of the info I share with you here will work for any credit scoring system. So don't feel like you're wasting your time reading this if you're interested in improving one of the other credit scores.

How FICO Scores are Rated

Everybody who cares to can figure out what goes into calculating their FICO credit score, and how much it contributes. Again, just to recap:

Payment history, 35%

Credit utilization, 30%

Length of credit history, 15%

New credit, 10%

Credit mix, 10%

The FICO algorithm is proprietary, which is short for they won't tell you exactly how it works.

Fine. Whatever. But they do tell you your final score, and it's easy to see if you did good.

At the end of it all, what you get is a single, three-digit number. And whether it's considered good or bad depends on what range it falls in.

Here's how FICO scores are generally rated by credit institutions.

SCORE RANGE	RATING
300-559	Poor
560-669	Fair
670-739	Good
740-799	Very Good
800-850	Excellent

So that's the long and short of your FICO credit score. Easy enough to understand with the right background info.

A Credit Report vs a Credit Score

I know that when I started out, I was a little confused. People kept talking about credit reports AND credit scores, and I didn't know what was what.

It turned out to be simple. A credit report is what is used to calculate your credit score. It's where the credit institutions keep tabs on your financial doings.

So any time you make a payment on a loan, open a new credit card, close a loan account, and myriad more things, they all get logged in your credit report.

In short, **a credit report is a logbook of your actual financial activity.**

FICO (and VantageScore too) then use your credit reports to calculate your credit score.

Credit reports?

As in plural?

Yes. You actually have all of three official credit reports. Why? Who knows.

Who Makes Your Credit Reports and When

Okay. So, I can't tell you why there had to be all of three credit reports, but I can tell you who makes them.

The US has three big-wig credit bureaus:

Equifax, Experian, and TransUnion.

Everybody has to jump when they say toad.

And each of the three makes its own credit report on you, so you always have three (potentially different!) credit reports.

This can and does complicate matters sometimes.

Not all credit institutions report to all three credit bureaus. So some of your financial info may be missing from some of your credit reports.

Then there's the issue of timing. The credit bureau receives data on you from your lenders, but may not update your credit report immediately.

At the end of it all, what your credit score reads heavily depends on three things:

> One, when it was calculated,

> Two, whether it used all three credit reports, or just one or two, and

> Three, if the credit reports used were up to date or not.

Annoying, I know. But that's how it works.

Sometimes it can seem like these guys are doing their best to put spikes in your tires.

But even with all this confusion, it's not that hard to estimate your current credit score. Which is what you need to do to figure out where you stand.

Heck, you may even be able to get your real credit score without spending a penny!

So go grab that cup of coffee and roll up your sleeves. We're finally getting down to work!

CHAPTER 3
ESTIMATING YOUR CURRENT CREDIT SCORE

You're itching to figure out what your credit score is right now.

Maybe you're a little scared, but you still want to know.

No. You *need* to know.

Because knowing your credit score will let you know exactly where you stand. You'll know just what kind of chance you have of getting that house loan, or that credit card.

And if things turn out worse than you thought, at least you'll be able to start fixing the situation.

But estimating your credit score means you need to have all your financial facts at the tips of your fingers.

The smartest way to do that is to get hold of your credit reports. All three of 'em.

Get those, and you're taking out all the guesswork. And the cleaner your facts, the cleaner your estimated score.

How to Get Your Credit Reports from the Three Credit Bureaus

Getting hold of your credit reports is actually quite simple. You have a right to ask for and receive your credit report from each of the three national bureaus.

The national bureaus are equally obliged by law to supply you with your credit report.

The best part? It's FREE.

You can get one free credit report from each agency per year. And they seem to understand that chasing after three different reports from three different places can be a hassle.

So the three credit bureaus have collaborated to set up a single, central point for us consumers. You can ask for and get all three credit reports here, in just a few minutes.

With this one, don't get duped. There is ONLY ONE OFFICIAL POINT to retrieve your legit credit reports:

www.annualcreditreport.com

You can order for all three credit reports at once. Or you can get them one by one. Up to you.

Whatever your choice, there are three ways you can do this:

- Visit the website, fill in the simple info required, and you'll have instant access to your credit reports.

- Call 1-877-322-8228 toll-free, and order your credit reports. You'll have them within 15 days.

- You can also order your credit reports online by filling out the Annual Credit Request Form available at: https://bit.ly/3356pRg. With this option you'll also have to wait 15 days to receive your credit reports.

You won't be have to fill in any lengthy, cumbersome info. It's a very quick list:

1. Your name

2. Your address

3. Your social security number, and

4. Your date of birth.

That's it. Oh, if you've moved in the last two years, you'll have to give them your previous address too.

But that's really not much to ask for, and you can get it done in 5 minutes.

Traditionally, you can get only one free credit report per year from each of the three bureaus.

But from 2020 through to 2026, you can get all of 6 free credit reports per year from the Equifax website: www.equifax.com (you can also call 1-866-349-5191).

And that's on top of the three regular credit reports you get, one from each agency.

All I can say is, go for it! It might be more than a little scary, I know. But take a deep breath, steel your nerves, and take the plunge.

The earlier you get those credit reports, the earlier you can work out your current score.

Know thy enemy, they say.

But your credit score doesn't have to be your enemy. You can turn it into your best friend.

And ultimately, that's why we're here :)

Getting an Accurate Estimate of Your Credit Score Range

Now here's the truth. Your banker, credit card provider, insurer and a few other folks can get your actual credit score whenever they need it.

But if *you* want your real, current FICO score, you're likely to have to pay for it. There may be ways to dodge that.

More on that in just a couple.

But before that. Even if you can't always access your actual FICO score for free, you can estimate it.

The estimate won't give you an actual score. Instead, it will give you a range in which your score lies. But for most purposes, that's plenty to go on.

There's a number of websites where you can get your FICO score estimate, but all of them are powered by myFico.com.(www.myfico.com/fico-credit-score-estimator/estimator) So you might as well go straight to the source.

And the process is very basic. MyFico will walk you through a series of questions about your credit and payment history.

You can try to answer these questions even without your credit reports on hand. But the info required is quite specific, and guesstimating can put your score off by several points.

So the best way to use this FICO score estimator is by having accurate, up-to-date financial info. And the only way you're going to do that is by getting those credit reports.

So go to annualcreditreport.com and get those credit reports coming your way.

Then you can give www.myFico.com 10 minutes of your time, and get a reasonably accurate estimate of your score range.

How to Get An Actual FICO Score For Free

Okay. So myFico is the go-to site for all things FICO. And if you're willing to pay for it, you can access your FICO score with any one of their monthly plans.

But even the cheapest of these monthly plans from myFico will set you back almost $20 per month.

Now I don't know about you, but I have better ways of spending that money.

But hold up. Did you know that you may be able to access your FICO score completely free of charge?

Yep. It's possible.

Here's the thing. FICO has an Open Access Program. They partnered with over 200 financial institutions and allowed them to let their clients see their FICO score for free.

Some financial and credit counseling programs will also let you access your credit score for free.

There's a lot of credit providers, like Discover and Commerce Bank, that will provide you with your FICO score for free every month. Go here for a full list : www.ficoscore.com/where-to-get-fico-scores

The catch is, of course, that you use one or more of their products.

If you're not signed up with any institution that offers free FICO scores, don't rush into it just to get access to yours. Ask yourself if it's really worth it.

But if you're already a member of an institution that lets you access your score, then skip the estimator, and get the straight-up facts. After all, it's free.

CHAPTER 4
UNDERSTANDING WHAT CAN
HURT YOUR CREDIT SCORE

I f you've sat there looking at your credit score, actual or estimated, congrats. You've jumped your first big hurdle.

It's not easy racking up the courage, sometimes. But now that you did it, you can move on :)

Remember, you can jump back to our convenient little table in chapter 3 to check where your score lies if you're not too sure.

If your score is rated excellent, well done, you! All you gotta do is keep it up. You're definitely doing great. But read on to see just what pitfalls to avoid.

You don't have too much to worry about if your score is very good or even just good. Chances are you don't have any debt collectors breathing down your neck or some such.

But there's still room for improvement and plenty of good reasons to get your score climbing higher.

And if yours turned out to be fair or poor, then we have a lot of work to do. The sooner we get to it, the sooner you'll be seeing some much-needed improvement.

So let's not waste any time. No matter how good or bad your score, the most important thing to understand is what can hurt it.

10 Myths About Which Financial Information Appears on Your Credit Reports

1. **I've got good savings in the bank, so my credit scores got to be good.**

It's great if you've got good money stashed up in your bank accounts. You never know when you'll need it.

But bank balances aren't a factor when your credit score is calculated.

So it doesn't matter whether you have just $1 or a million bucks in there. Your credit score won't be the least bit affected.

2.   **But I was late on that loan payment over a year ago!!**

Okay, so you missed just the one payment on your house loan. You *did* pay it up, of course, but you were a few weeks late.

It was like 15 months ago, give or take. Doesn't really amount to much, does it, on my credit score?

Wrong, unfortunately. It really does count. Negative information can stay on your credit reports for up to 7 years.

True, it will carry less weight as time passes. But it will still carry weight and keep dragging your score downwards.

3.   **I got debit and prepaid cards to build up my score.**

Debit and prepaid cards are great. You don't have to worry about spending more than what you have.

But if you applied for one hoping to improve your credit score, bad news. There is no credit involved, so they just don't count toward your credit score. At all.

4. **I don't have any debt, so my credit score must be good.**

Not necessarily. If you finally paid your debt off after a bad bout of credit, you won't see any improvement in your credit score immediately. It will take months, if not years.

And if you're debt-free because you had to declare bankruptcy, that's even worse. Because bankruptcy drags your credit score down hard.

5. **Getting married will merge my score with my better half.**

Nope. Simply not true. Your credit history and credit score will still be yours, even after you get married.

Any joint accounts with your spouse will affect both your credit scores, but that's where it stops. All your individual financial records remain as before.

6. If I keep checking my credit score, it will go down.

Absolutely not true. You can check your credit score as often as you like, and it won't change one iota because of that.

Just be sure that you're using credit scoring services, not mortgage lenders. Checking your credit score through a mortgage lender *can* impact your score.

7. I need to be rich to have a good credit score...

Again, another big fat lie. Credit scores really aren't about your income, at least not directly.

So it doesn't matter whether you're a 6-figure executive or a supermarket attendant. Your income isn't a factor when calculating your credit score.

What *does* count is how responsibly you spend the income that you do have. Like paying your bills on time, and not borrowing more than you can afford.

8. Don't let them scare ya. It takes a loooong time for a credit score to go bad.

I hate to break it to you, but bad financial habits or a few unintentional mistakes can ruin a good score in just half a year.

Not all that long, is it?

Take a simple example. If your account is past due date by 6-months, it will be charged off. Just a couple of chargeoffs or collections can kill your score.

9. Paying off a collection debt will improve my score.

Collection agencies are good at making you believe paying off is the only and best alternative. But it may not be. More on this in chapter 6.

And even if you do pay it off, you'll only see an improvement on your score long-term. Short-term, it won't change a thing.

10. It takes 7 years to improve a credit score. Why am I even bothering??

Okay. This one is yes and no.

It's true that a lot of negative information stays on your credit reports (and affects your credit score) for a good seven years.

But this information loses weight as it ages. So it won't affect your score as bad in year 2 or 3 as it did in year 1.

Plus, even if your negative accounts haven't fallen off, good behavior counts. Paying your bills on time and having reasonable debt will earn you points.

The Truth About How Your Financial Actions Are Interpreted by FICO

That may not be all of the myths about credit scores out there. But we've covered the more common ones. And reading this book through to the end will likely dispel the rest.

And now that we have the confusing stuff out of the way, I just wanted to give you a quick recap of how FICO really calculates your credit score.

Your payment history matters the most. It accounts for 35% of your total score. So even a single missed payment can do a fair amount of damage.

Next is your credit utilization. The next 30% is based on how much of your total available credit you're using. Too much is obviously not a great idea.

The length of your credit history contributes 15% to your final score. A long history is better, but only if it's a good one.

Applying for new credit can have an effect on your credit score, but counts for only 10% of the total.

Credit mix gives you the last 10%. FICO considers people with a mix of loan types as 'better' than those with just one type of credit. Of course, this is as long as all the loans are well managed.

Ultimately, you want to use your common sense and keep things clean. Take out loans, but only when you need them, and no more than you can afford to pay back.

Almost every misstep will be recorded on your credit reports. And once there, it can pull your credit score down for up to seven years.

Seven years is a crazy long time to pay for a seemingly small mistake. So it's important to know what the most common ones are.

The 7 Most Common Causes of a Bad Credit Score

1. Late payments

This is probably the most common score-killing item on this, or any other, list.

Sometimes life pushes you into a corner, and you just can't make a loan payment on time. Unfortunately, FICO will still punish you for it, regardless of your reasons.

2. Missed credit card payments

Not paying up your credit balances in full and on time is another way to lower your score quite quickly.

This one also gets noted under your payment history. And remember, this category is a solid 35% of your total score.

3. Charge-offs

When your lender decides you're not interested in paying off your debt, they'll write you off.

A chargeoff sends all the wrong messages to any future lenders, telling them you can't be trusted. It will also cost you A LOT of points on your FICO score.

4. Collection accounts

Sometimes a lender will sell your account to a third party (the dreaded collection agency) if you've defaulted on your loan for too long.

A collection account is another massive score-killing item. And the effects are very long-lasting: your credit score will be limping seven long years.

5. Using too much credit

Having credit cards and using them is great. And that won't damage your score in and of itself. Quite the opposite.

But if you use too much of your total available credit, lenders can get the message that you're desperate for cash. Use tops 30%, no more than that.

6. Too many requests for new credit

Making too many so-called 'hard' inquiries can also send your credit score sliding downhill.

Now, this doesn't mean you can't ask for new credit. It's about the *how* you do it.

Say you're shopping for a home loan. You ask 5 different mortgage lenders in the space of two weeks to get a comparison.

That's cool. That counts as only one inquiry to FICO. No big deal.

But then you ask about a new credit card, a home loan, AND a car loan, all in the space of one month.

That's telling the big guns that you're living over your limits, and are a high risk. They won't be in a hurry to lend you their precious money.

7. **Not having a credit history, or having a short one**

It may seem unfair, but having a short credit history works against you, not for.

What?? I've been so careful with my money, I've never even had to take a loan!!

Yep. I get it.

But FICO's point of view is that if you've never taken a loan, they have no way of knowing how you'll handle the payments.

And if you've owned a credit card for just a year, that's not a guarantee that you know how to handle it (and your expenditures) either.

Are you to be trusted? Or will you simply misuse the money?

So there you have it. Having a minimal credit history or none at all can work against you.

But fear not. There are ways around this one. We have a whole chapter dedicated to solving this little problem. Just keep reading.

If any of these things ring a bell, then you know what's happened to keep your score from being all pretty and shiny.

Unfortunately, there isn't much I can do to change a bad financial situation.

But what I can do for you is help you figure out how to stop things from getting any worse.

And I even have a few tricks up my sleeve to show you how to reduce the impact of some of that score-killing stuff.

That means you can start improving your score right away. Right now.

And all you folks with amazing credit scores, keep your eyes peeled.

You just might find yourself that 'Aha, didn't know that one!' moment in here :)

CHAPTER 5
THE FASTEST WAYS TO MAXIMIZE YOUR CREDIT SCORE

So we finally get to it.

You've worked out just what that three-digit number really means, and you know where it came from.

You also know just how it can affect you, and why it's literally a must to make sure yours is in good standing.

Let's dive straight into it.

I'm not going to give you general do-it-like-this guidelines to keep your score good in this chapter.

I'm more interested in helping you make a few crucial financial decisions that you've likely been wondering about.

The correct approach to making these decisions is not set in stone. It just depends on your personal situation, and I want to help you get some perspective.

Credit Reports Often Have Score-Killing Errors!

Those credit reports, all three of them?

Yep, the ones from Equifax, Experian, and TransUnion.

They are made by human beings. Everyday, fallible human beings like me and you.

And that means they make mistakes!

Sometimes big ones, sometimes small ones. But the mistakes happen. Frequently enough.

Did you know that even a small error like a misspelled name or address, or a wrong birthday, can affect your credit score?

And that's even before we get to actual financial data, like wrong payment dates on your loans, or a credit card balance wrongly marked as unpaid.

Once you get hold of your credit reports, make it a point to check them thoroughly for errors. From top to bottom.

Dispute Every Mistake on Your Credit Reports

So if and when you do discover errors on any of your credit reports, DISPUTE THEM!!

No matter how small or big the error is. If you are reasonably sure it's an error, it's your legal right to have it fixed.

So if you find an error on one of your credit reports,

> Dispute the error with the credit reporting agency in question. That's Equifax, Experian, or TransUnion. Explain in writing what you think is wrong and why. If you have them, include documents to support your point.

> Dispute the same error with the company that provided the info in the first place. That could be your bank, credit card company, insurance provider, or whoever.

Nine out of ten times, the error is made by the credit reporting agency. But they're obliged by law to correct it if it holds water, and they usually will.

Getting rid of errors can raise your score just a little, or a whole lot. Really depends on what the errors are.

Unless, of course, the error worked in your favor. It might be tempting not to report one of these. But it could turn around and bite you later if somebody (like a court) starts digging.

Sort Out Your Credit Cards The Smart Way

Having a credit card or two is useful. It's a major convenience. And your credit cards won't hurt your credit score at all if you just manage them smart.

Watch how much credit you utilize.

It doesn't matter how many credit cards you have. Could be one, or could be seven.

Ideally, you should be using no more than 30% of your total available credit.

Here's a simple example. Let's say you have four credit cards, and your available credit is $10,000, spread among the cards.

You shouldn't rack up a balance of more than $3000 at the end of the month, which is the 30% we just talked about. And less than 30% is even better.

And it doesn't matter whether all of it is on just one card, or spread among two or more of the cards.

FICO looks at your *total* available credit.

It doesn't matter if you maxed out one of your credit cards if you've used less than 30% of your total credit limit.

If your current credit utilization ratio is over 30%, don't panic. Instead, make a plan to **gradually cut the ratio down to where you need it to be.**

This could mean getting rid of some non-essential expenses (and you'd be surprised what you can live without if you just choose to do so!).

You can also consider opening new lines of credit and closing old ones.

Have a proper go at the section below to decide whether these options can help you.

How Closing an Account Can Affect You

Sometimes, people think that closing an old credit account can raise your credit score.

Usually, not true.

See, the first thing closing a credit account is going to do is lower your credit limit. And that will immediately affect your credit utilization ratio.

Closing a credit account will increase your credit utilization ratio. And this will decrease your credit score.

So the only good reason for voluntarily closing a credit account is if you're really not using it, and it charges you an annual or monthly fee.

On the other hand, let's say you have an old credit account that's no longer in use, but is in good standing. Say it's a student or housing loan that you paid off exactly as agreed.

Having this account open, even though you're not using it, will contribute nicely to your credit history.

If you close it, you lose the positive effect it had on your credit score within a few years. So again, unless it's costing you money to maintain, leave it be.

Whether to Open a New Line of Credit or Not

Getting yourself a new credit card may or may not work to your advantage.

Let's say your credit score is generally in good shape and you don't have any bad history anywhere.

Applying for a single new credit card will drop your score by a few points, but it's negligible.

On the other hand, having a new credit card increases your credit limit. This lowers your credit utilization ratio and raises your credit score.

Just be sure not to apply for more than one credit type in 30 days.

So even if you want a home loan *and* a credit card, apply for the one first.

Leave the other for later on.

How to Handle Credit Card Limits and Balances

I risk stating the obvious here. But if you have only one credit card, do whatever you safely can to avoid maxing it out.

Do your best to use less than 30% of the credit available to you on that card.

If you've got more than one credit card, maxing one of them out may not do any damage, as long as you pay the balance in full and on time.

Actually, no matter how many credit cards you have, there is one golden rule.

Always pay back your credit card balances in full by the due date.

If you find you can't keep your credit utilization ratio down, *consider raising the credit limit on one or more of your cards.*

As long as you don't use any more money than you did before, this will bring your credit utilization ratio down. And that will show positively on your credit score quite quickly.

What You Need To Know About Debt Consolidation

Debt consolidation can be a really good solution to making your debts more manageable.

Done the right way, it can also raise your credit score in the long term.

Combining several of your debts into one has its appeals.

> Having several debt accounts makes it more likely you'll make a mistake, like missing a payment. This will hurt your credit score.

> Consolidating your debt can save you money. Say you have a credit card that charges you 15% interest. Consolidating into a new loan with a lower interest rate can save you much-needed money.

Now let's look at what happens to your credit score when you consolidate your debts.

Short-term, your score will suffer a bit. It will take a hit from the new credit inquiry that you had to make to open the new loan account.

Opening a new credit account also temporarily lowers your credit score. That's because it lowers your average credit account age.

But then there's the real benefit.

Of course, this assumes that you actually use the consolidation account to pay your debts off, and don't rack up new ones.

As time passes and you keep making on-time payments to your debt consolidation account, it improves your payment history.

And remember, that's a cool 35% of your total score.

So if you're willing to take a short-term dip in your score, you can get a substantial improvement over the next couple of years.

What NOT To Do When Fixing Your Credit Score

We've talked about all the things you can do to quickly get your score going up instead of down.

Not every strategy will work for everyone. Assess your own situation critically, and think carefully before you do something.

Because ultimately, every financial activity that is related to credit gets onto your credit reports, one way or another.

Then there's a few no-nos when it comes to improving your credit score.

These are the things you really shouldn't do because they'll cause you nothing but grief.

Don't procrastinate. Repairing your credit can seem impossible, especially when you're in a tight spot. But you've got to start somewhere. And the sooner you start, the sooner things get better.

Don't dispute everything on your credit reports. This is an approach often taken by credit repair agencies. But if you dispute everything, you will simply lose credibility. Your claim will be dismissed.

And you could hurt your score even further if you end up losing some of the positive info on your credit reports.

Don't miss some payments in favor of others. Things can get really difficult sometimes. But missing on payments is only going to lower your score, not improve it.

The only time you shouldn't make a payment is if the account has already been charged-off. Paying on a charged-off account will reopen it, lowering your score even further.

> **Avoid the balance transfer game.** Transferring balances from one credit card to another to avoid making a payment is a deadly game you're playing with time.

This tactic does nothing to solve your debt problem. It only delays the inevitable. Instead, look for real solutions that will raise your credit score AND lower your debt.

> **Don't give up on credit cards altogether.** Canceling a credit card will only worsen your credit score, especially if the card has a balance on it.

And not having or using any credit cards at all will hurt your ability to get new loans and other credit cards later on.

Plus, using a credit card the right way will actually improve your credit score.

> **Don't rush into hiring a credit repair company.** Think very carefully before going down this road.

Most credit repair companies are unscrupulous. They'll promise you miracles that they just can't deliver. You'll only waste even more of your hard-earned money.

In my opinion, you're best off doing your credit repair on your own. It may be unpleasant, and it will cost you some time.

But it's not rocket science. And it will teach you how to manage your finances better in the process.

If you do decide to hire a credit repair firm, please read through the next chapter first. I've given tips on how to best find a reputable one that won't rip you off.

If you need to go over this chapter an extra time or two, please do. Better to be sure that what you're doing is the best thing you could be doing.

Chances are, even if your credit score isn't bad to begin with, you've still picked up a little something till this point.

Sometimes, it's a case of beating the system at its own game.

When I first started out, I was happy using my single credit card because it was enough for me.

I had no idea that having multiple lines and types of credit was actually a good thing. Who would have thought?? Totally counter-intuitive, at least for me.

But back to the main topic. Even if your score is not too shabby, you'll be wanting to push it up those extra few points.

It's not hard either and doesn't cost you much except a few minutes of your time here and there.

But before we get there, I want to take you through the pros and cons of using a credit repair company.

And if you need a loan but can't get one because you simply don't have a credit score, no worries. I've got you covered too.

CHAPTER 6
ARE CREDIT REPAIR AGENCIES WORTH IT?

See, if you're thinking of using a credit repair company, it means you're in a tight situation, and you're really worried.

Credit repair companies will often take advantage of that. They may not lie to you outright, but they know how to pitch their stuff just right to hook you.

You may come away soothed, thinking your troubles are sorted.

But more often than not, they won't be able to do any more for you than you could for yourself. The only difference is that you'll be paying them money to do it.

When To Use Credit Repair Agencies

Before you hire a credit repair agency, ask yourself one simple question.

Do you really have that much work that needs to be done on your credit report?

Credit repair companies usually work by doing whatever possible to remove derogatory remarks on your credit reports. So they'll be looking to deal with stuff like:

> Bankruptcies
>
> Tax liens
>
> Charge-offs

They'll set up a plan to dispute errors and negotiate with creditors to remove those items from your credit reports.

The first step may be to validate information, after which they'll be sending letters to the relevant companies to dispute wrongly recorded information.

And these are things you can easily do yourself.

The other thing credit repair agencies may do is send cease-and-desist letters to credit collection agencies on your behalf. And again, this is something you can take care of on your own.

They may also try to get you to open up new credit accounts in a bid to raise your credit score. But you've already seen that this may not be the best solution.

Negotiating with your creditors may sound scary, but they're human beings, just like you.

It's in their interest to have their money paid back without resorting to debt collection agencies. They'll only be happy to come to a settlement with you.

In short, there's nothing a credit repair agency can do that you can't do yourself.

If you have just one or two errors to take care of, you're honestly best off doing it yourself.

You can get hold of your credit reports 100% free, and disputing those errors isn't a Gargantuan task either.

In a situation where you have a really bad credit history, you may feel that it's more efficient to get a credit repair company to do the heavy lifting for you.

But ask yourself if the money you're paying them isn't better spent paying your debts back.

Some credit repair companies charge by each derogatory mark removed. And that could cost you anywhere from $35 to $750 per mark.

Others will charge you a monthly fee, starting from $30 and up.

You're smart. I know it. So do the math.

Still think it's worth it? Go ahead, be my guest.

But if you're reconsidering (like most of us end up doing), then all you have to do is dedicate a few hours of your time to sort your credit issues out.

If you take it step by step, it's surprisingly straightforward.

Don't Get Duped by Unscrupulous Credit Repair Companies

There are plenty of scam companies out there, just waiting to take advantage of you.

But not all of them are shady. There are some legit ones too.

How can you tell?

There's a few things to look out for. If a credit repair company:

Promises you it can legally make a new credit identity for you

Guarantees you an improved credit score

Requests you to pay before it provides its services

Claims it can remove accurate negative info from your credit reports

turn around and run like hell.

These are all red flags telling you the company doesn't do things above the board. They'll take your money without delivering results.

Worse still, they could land you in serious trouble with the law.

There's No Such Thing as a Government-Sanctioned Agency

Wouldn't it be nice if there were a few companies okayed by government? That way, you could be sure you're getting decent, legit services, probably at a reasonable fee.

But there's really no such thing. Period.

In fact, the Federal Trade Commission sees the idea of credit repair companies in general as a farce.

So if you want to use a credit repair company, you'll have to do your background checks by your lonesome. No two ways about it.

How to Verify a Credit Repair Company

Don't be in a hurry to throw in the towel, though.

To be honest, I kind of agree with the FTC. There's really no reason to hire someone to do what you can easily do yourself.

But if you're just not up to it, here's how to vet credit repair companies.

> Check them out on the Better Business Bureau (www.bbb.org)

> Search the Consumer Complaint Database (www.consumerfinance.gov/data-research/consumer-complaints) to see how your chosen credit repair company is faring

> Visit a free credit counseling agency (and there are many around) to ask if they know of a reputable credit repair agency

Check out as many review websites as possible to see what people are saying.

As you scour the net, beware of rosy reviews written in funny English: these are usually paid reviews done by cheap content writers.

List of Things to Do BEFORE You Hire a Credit Repair Company

So here's a quick recap. Go through this checklist BEFORE signing up with a credit repair company to avoid getting scammed.

Credit repair agencies are bound by law to charge you only *after* delivering their services. So if you're being asked to pay upfront, leave it be.

Make sure they give you a written copy of the contract, with all the details included.

Check that you can cancel the contract within the first three days of signing, at no cost. This is also a condition set by law.

Check the company out on the Better Business Bureau (www.bbb.org) and the Consumer Complaint Database to see what people are saying.

And I can't stress this point enough. If the company is promising you guaranteed results or claims to be able to legally set you up with a new credit profile, RUN. Fast.

Such companies are only interested in taking your not-so-plentiful money, and will not deliver any decent results.

Heck, even a reputable credit repair agency can only do so much. So watch out.

CHAPTER 7
WHAT IF I DON'T HAVE A CREDIT SCORE?

First off, don't stress. There's lots of people that don't have a credit score.

It doesn't make you inferior in any way. It simply means you've never taken out any official credit.

And there are plenty of people that have what's called a 'thin' credit file.

If you've only ever taken out the one loan, that's you.

If you have never taken a long-term loan but have one credit card, that's also you.

Fear not.

There are things you can do to build up a credit score quite quickly. And since you're actively working to build it, you'll be able to do things just right.

So you'll be building an *excellent* credit score, not just *a* credit score.

Use a Thin Credit File To Your Advantage

This one can be a bit of a paradox. You need to take out credit to build up your credit score.

But because your credit file is 'thin', lenders don't have enough info to base their decisions on. And so you can't get any credit, so your file remains thin.

Bit of a bummer, isn't it.

But there's over 62 million Americans in this boat. Either they don't have a credit file at all, or it's so thin, it's as good as nonexistent.

And if you're part of this group, credit institutions definitely want your business. Because it's people like you that put bread on their tables.

There are easy, quick ways to build up a credit file, even from zero.

And you know the best part?

You know just what counts for a good credit score, and what earns you a bad one.

At this point, you probably don't have any bad credit history. So instead of worrying about fixing your credit score, you get to build one from scratch.

If you've gone through every chapter in this book so far, then you know exactly what tactics to use to get to the top of FICO's scoring system.

And even if you're interested in another credit score like VantageScore, most of these strategies still hold water.

5 Things You Can Do To Build a Good Credit Score Fast

There are a few easy, practical ways to fatten up your credit score. You won't get yourself a credit score overnight, but it doesn't take forever either.

Do some of the stuff on the list below, and you'll have yourself a good credit score, going on excellent, in a year.

> **Get a boost from someone else's credit history.** If there's someone you know and trust financially (and who trusts you), you can piggyback off of them.

Become an authorized user on their credit card account, and you automatically benefit from their good credit history and score.

But watch out! If your benefactor has any negative financial activity on their credit reports, it will reflect on you too.

> **Apply for a secured credit card.** It works just like a normal credit card. It comes with a credit limit and will be accepted by most merchants.

The difference is that it requires a refundable security deposit when opening your account. The deposit is normally the equivalent of your credit limit.

Your limit can be anything, from just a couple hundred to several thousand bucks.

Either way, make sure to pay it in full and on time at the end of the month. Otherwise, you'll incur interest, just like with a normal credit card.

Many banks that offer secured credit cards will let you upgrade to an unsecured one after 6 months.

So manage your secured credit card well and you'll soon have other lines of credit accessible to you.

Get a credit-builder loan. These are loans designed specifically to build your credit history. You can find them at credit unions and community financial institutions.

Usually, the money you 'borrow' is held by the lender in a savings account, and will be returned to you once you pay off the loan in full.

So look out for short-term loans (24 months is a good starting point). Also make sure your payment history will be reported to at least one of the three credit bureaus.

Get your rental bills reported to the credit bureaus. If you are living in a rented home, make your monthly rent payments work for you.

There are many services like Rental Kharma (rentalkharma.com) and RentTrack (www.renttrack.com/renters) that will report all your rent payments to the credit bureaus on your behalf.

Not all these services are free, so be sure to read the fine print before you sign up.

Join Experian Boost and UltraFico. These are programs designed to help people build up their credit scores.

Experian Boost collects data that doesn't normally show up on your credit report, like utility payments and banking history.

So if you have a good payment history with your everyday bills, you can take advantage of Experian Boost to build up your credit score.

UltraFico works on the same principles. It mainly relies on your banking history to help build up your score.

If you go for UltraFico, avoid overdrafts, pay your bills through your bank account, and have a savings cushion to make the most of it.

CHAPTER 8
HOW TO GO FROM A NOT-SO-BAD CREDIT SCORE TO AN EXCELLENT ONE

It doesn't matter if you've had a credit score for a good long while, or you're just starting out.

Either way, it pays to keep that number as high as possible.

We've already looked at practical ways you can fix up a not-so-good credit score.

And those same tactics apply even when you're building your score from scratch.

The way I see it, if you've taken the trouble to build up an excellent credit score, you definitely don't want it sliding back down.

It's okay for it to take a minor hit every now and then. Like if you make a new credit inquiry, or close an old credit card that is costing you annual fees.

And you certainly know to avoid the stuff that will send your score plummeting. Like missing payments, or utilizing more than 30% of your available credit at any one time.

But there are little things you can do to make it easier to keep track of your finances. Especially when it comes to money you've borrowed and will have to pay back.

Use Credit Monitoring Services

One of the easiest ways of keeping track of your credit reports (and therefore credit score!) is to use a credit monitoring service.

These services work by tracking changes in your credit activity. They'll notify you if a new account has been opened, or a large purchase made.

Credit monitoring services are also invaluable when it comes to detecting identity theft and fraud.

Criminals can use a stolen credit card number to make illegal online purchases, or file fake Medicare and social security claims.

If this goes undetected, your credit score will plummet before you realize anything has happened.

Some of these services are free, others charge a fee. Some offer only basic features, others are very comprehensive.

Even the paid ones are usually reasonably priced. A few bucks spent on monitoring your credit monthly can save you thousands later on. Not to mention untold frustration.

Get a Handle on Your Bill Payments

This is where many of us often go wrong. It's *so* easy to forget to pay a bill, especially when you have several.

You can help yourself by keeping reminders on your phone calendar for all due dates. That way, you'll get an alert for every single bill, and never miss one accidentally.

Another option is to consolidate all your bill payments to a credit card. That way, all the bills will automatically get paid off as and when due. All you have to do is pay off a single credit card balance every month.

The same idea works with having your bills come off of a bank account.

As long as you keep the account balance high enough, the rest will go like clockwork.

Keep Your Credit Utilization Within Limits

This is a simple rule to remember. Never use more than 30% of your total available credit.

If you need more credit (and can afford it), apply for a new credit line, or raise the limits on your existing credit cards.

And if you need more credit but cannot realistically manage it, then it's time to tighten your belt. Cut out some of your unnecessary expenses (I'm not pointing fingers, we all have them).

Limit Your Credit Inquiries

When things are going well, and hopefully they are, you may find yourself thinking about a larger purchase. And this means a new loan.

You cannot dodge making a credit inquiry altogether. But remember how the scoring system works, and be smart about it.

Don't make too many credit inquiries for different credit types all at once.

Asking five different banks for a new credit card counts for only one inquiry. But asking about a car loan, mortgage, and credit card in the space of one week is a score-killing move.

And there you have it. Seemingly simple things, but people often don't think to do them. Yet they can do a lot to help you manage your finances and build a better credit score.

Use these handy tips to your advantage, and they'll do more than just help you build an excellent score.

They'll help you plan for your money more efficiently. And they'll go a long way toward making sure a bad credit score, if you have one, is steadily rectified.

FINAL NOTES

The Sooner You Up Your Credit Score, The Sooner You'll Start Paying Less for More

That wasn't so bad now, was it?

All the big-wigs at Forbes and the like can make it sound like you need to be Einstein to figure out how credit scores work.

But it's actually as simple as taking a couple of hours off to read a little book. Like this one… :)

So I'd like to say thank you. I want you to know I wrote this book to help people, and I really appreciate you taking the time to read it.

It means a lot to me.

I still wish something like this had been around when I was trying to figure out how to bump up my credit score.

But look on the bright side. You can piggyback off of my experiences and get things done right from the word go.

No need to waste valuable time and get frustrated.

To sum it all up, having a great credit score is mostly about being smart with your finances. And we went through lots of how-to's here.

And just a little bit about knowing exactly what to do so you can use the system to your advantage.

Although this little bit *can* make a big difference.

So if you haven't yet ordered your credit reports and made a credit repair/improvement to-do list, what are you waiting for??

Remember, your score won't improve overnight. No matter how much you might want it to. It just takes a while.

So the sooner you get started, the sooner you'll see the improvement you're looking for.

And that's when you'll find doors that have previously been closed will magically open for you.

No more rejected loan applications or sky-high interest rates.

You'll have the financial freedom you've always wanted.

And you'll have a chance to do the things that really matter. Like getting that wedding you've always dreamed of, or finally buying a home.

Improving Your Score Is Not Hard. It Just Takes a Bit of Effort.

Please don't be mad at me for saying this so much. But it's true. Raising your credit score really isn't rocket science.

All you need to do is take a little time to understand how credit scores work. If you can do that, you'll know what to do, and what not to do. And why.

And in this case, knowledge is true power. You'll have 100% control over what goes into your credit reports.

And THAT means 100% control over what that all-important credit score reads.

After all, isn't that why you've kept reading this? :)

You can do it, and you will see results.

Your credit score will rise and you'll be in a better position to do the things you want to do.

It's a process, and you now know you're up for it.

Build a great score, and best of luck in your journey!

YOUR FREE GIFT

If you haven't done so already, please accept my **FREE bonus gifts** of below special PDF Cheat sheet and Checklist.

"Everything You Need to Know to Check Your Credit Score" (Cheat Sheet)

"15 Things That You Can Do To Improve Your Credit Score". (Checklist)

The Cheat sheet will guide you with an easy, step-by-step way to check your credit score and the Checklist will show you a list of simple, practical things that you can do to improve your credit score drastically!

Get it Here:

https://BookHip.com/BFBFTT

ALSO BY RACHEL MERCER

Check out the best-selling first book in the *Smart Personal Money Management Series, "How to Budget & Manage Your Money".* This book will teach you to master your money with proven money management techniques to protect your credit score and to control your finances.

HOW TO BUDGET & MANAGE YOUR MONEY

Financial Planning Books for Beginners
How to Save Money Faster, Pay Off Debt and Control Your Finances

Go here to see it on Amazon:
www.amazon.com/dp/B086DK2DXV

What people are saying about *"How to Budget & Manage Your Money"*:

- "With practice sheets, it should be a required high school senior life skills course. I read the book cover to cover. I would love to see this book implemented as a required high school course… This book is a good blueprint for financial success for almost anyone." Carolyn Overcash (Amazon Reader)

- "More than what is stated. I like that she had a novel approach to managing money...I like the bigger perspective on why people should budget…" Jamie Bee (Amazon Top 50 Reviewer)

- "Wish I had this book 3 years ago. It is worth buying and practicing the budgeting advice given. I recommend this book to everyone. If you need great money advice, this book is the best." Wayne Russell (Amazon Reader)

- "An amazing book on budget. A detailed explanation on how to make a budget and stick to it." (Amazon Reader)

THANK YOU

Did you enjoy this book?

Then may I ask you a small favor?

Thank you for taking a chance and purchasing this book.

I really hope this book was helpful to you and hope you found some benefit in reading this book.

If you enjoyed the book and found it useful, would you consider leaving a review on Amazon?

If you could take 2 minutes and **leave a review on Amazon**, I would truly appreciate it!

Reviews on Amazon are critically important and really do make a difference for other readers to make a decision and for indie authors like myself to spread the word and to reach new readers.

I read all of my reviews and I would really love to hear your thoughts.

Here is the URL address of the book page on Amazon to leave your review.

https://www.amazon.com/product-review/B08GQJX7DS

You can also leave a review on **Goodreads** or share it on **Facebook**, **Instagram, Twitter, Youtube, Pinterest** and share with your **friends and family members** if you liked the book.

Thank you for taking the time and I really appreciate your support!